The Successful Airbnb Rental Arbitrage Millionaire

The **New and Up-to-Date Guide** on How to **Quit Your Job** and Become an Airbnb Super-Host with a **Fully Automated** & **Highly Profitable** Property, **without Owning any Property**. Including **Industry Secrets** from **Experts.**

Frank Walter

Introduction

Putting a significant amount of money into the buying of a property is not an easy feat.

What if you could still make humongous profits from real estate without actually spending money on any property?

That'd be great, right?

Short-term rental arbitrage is a less well-known but successful approach for making money on platforms like Airbnb and VRBO. To be successful with this method, you do not need to own real estate.

Arbitrage is a continuation of the "buy low, sell high" philosophy that underpins all businesses.

To give you an example, a bottle of water with a single serving purchased in bulk at a store may cost one dollar. If you buy the identical bottle from a vending machine, though, you should expect to pay at least $2 for it. If you buy the same bottle at a stadium or an airport, you might have to pay $5 for it.

Although the product has not been altered in any way, the manner in which it is delivered can have a substantial impact on its value.

Arbitrage in the rental market works the same way. On a one-year lease, the cost of renting an apartment might be $2,000 each month, or roughly $67 per day. However, if it were rented out on a per-night basis, the price could be substantially higher.

I discovered a way to capitalize on this pricing differential by negotiating a lease on an apartment, house, or condominium and then subletting the space to others on a weekly basis through apps like Airbnb and VRBO.

After that, I keep the difference, which is known as a premium in the industry.

You can profit from the pricing discrepancies that exist between short-term rentals and long-term rentals by using Airbnb rental arbitrage.

Whether you reside in the middle of nowhere or in the heart of a bustling city, acquiring a home with the goal of running it as an Airbnb business can be an excellent way to generate passive income.

In this book, I'll walk you through the steps of launching a real estate rental business utilizing this method, as well as where to seek for opportunities.

I will also show you the pros and cons of this business as well as how to get a landlord that would be willing to go through with this model with you.

I will also show you how to get the perfect properties for your Airbnb rental arbitrage business in order to ensure profitability.

Let's get to it, shall we?

Chapter One

Airbnb Basics: What Is Airbnb?

Airbnb (Air Bed and Breakfast) is a business that allows property owners to rent out their unoccupied rooms and flats to travelers who need a place to stay.

Travelers can rent a place that can accommodate a large group of people at the same time, a common space with separate rooms, or the entire property for themselves.

In 2008, two industrial designers named Brian Chesky and Joe Gebbia moved to San Francisco and founded the company that would become known as Airbnb.

Because they couldn't pay their loft rent at the time, the two decided that renting out their apartment to those who couldn't find motels to stay in while attending trade shows in the area would be the best option for them to make up the difference.

They served a home-cooked breakfast in the morning and forced their guests to sleep on air mattresses placed up in the flat's living room as sleeping arrangements.

Since then, Airbnb has grown to become one of the most successful peer-to-peer rental services accessible.

What exactly does Airbnb does?

The cornerstone of Airbnb is a peer-to-peer business model. This makes it simple to understand, simple to implement, and often more beneficial for both parties.

The concept also allows you to tailor and personalize the experience you deliver for your consumers in any way you see proper.

Who Makes Airbnb Reservations?

It is critical to have a thorough understanding of your demographic before selecting a new booking site. Millennials are projected to account for over 60% of all guests who have ever booked on Airbnb.

The typical Airbnb tourist is a young individual in their twenties or thirties who is technologically savvy. These visitors show a strong preference for staying in authentic, community-oriented lodging.

They believe that staying in Airbnb-listed lodgings will provide them with more opportunity to participate in cultural activities, which is one of the most essential things for them to do when traveling.

The fact that not everyone who travels can afford to stay in a hotel, let alone find a hotel room in a crowded urban area, contributes significantly to the industry's growing popularity. Airbnb provides a handy and, in many circumstances, less expensive option for them to consider.

How Does the Airbnb Platform Work for Hosts?

Whether you manage a bed and breakfast or a business that rents out vacation homes, your reservation system can be integrated straight into Airbnb.

Because many of these APIs can sync content, pricing, and availability, you'll be able to control your content on Airbnb.

Additionally, your Airbnb bookings will be automatically linked to your booking engine. If you already use Airbnb, several of these platforms will connect your existing listings, ensuring that you preserve your host ranking and status even if you transfer platforms.

Many of them offer free interfaces; the only fee is Airbnb's commission, which ranges from 3% to 5% each booking (depending on the cancellation policy you choose).

Questions and Answers for Airbnb Hosts

> ➤ How much is this going to cost?

Bookings on Airbnb are frequently half the price of bookings on other listing sites because acquisition fees can be as low as 3%. Furthermore, Airbnb is liable for any payment card processing fees!

> ➤ How will I be paid?

Airbnb's online payment mechanism protects the security of each and every transaction. When a reservation is made, the guest's credit card is promptly debited, and the host is reimbursed within 24 hours of the guest's arrival. It is up to you to decide how you want to get paid; you can use direct deposit, PayPal, or any number of other options.

NOTE: Airbnb does not collect taxes automatically.

➤ Do my rates need to be reduced to stay competitive on Airbnb?

When compared to the cost of a single hotel room, the rates offered by Airbnb for renting out an entire home are usually equivalent to, if not lower than, the rates offered by hotels. Nonetheless, there are a few luxury homes on the list.

Airbnb Host Prerequisites

If you want to become an Airbnb host, you should know that the company needs you to make at least 30 days of your listing's year-long calendar open for booking at all times. Before you associate a listing, make sure the associated rate type has a price for at least 30 days.

Airbnb Hosting Rules

The following are additional qualifications for becoming an Airbnb host:

> ➤ Make certain that your guests have the bare needs, if not more. You must supply each guest with their own supply of toilet paper, soap, linens, and at least one towel and pillow.
>
> You are responsible for providing anything further, and I urge you to offer something extra to get a good rating as a host!

> ➤ You must be attentive. Please react to queries and reservation requests within 24 hours of receiving them.

> ➤ Please respond to any reservation requests as soon as possible. Simply told, the sooner the better!

> ➤ Please do not cancel. Airbnb takes host cancellations extremely seriously. They understand that travel plans are dependent on accommodations, which is why cancellations are frowned upon.

➢ Maintain a high level of quality consistently to ensure that you obtain a high grade.

Chapter Two

What Exactly Is Airbnb Rental Arbitrage?

Aside from directly owning property and renting it out on a short-term basis, Airbnb has grown since 2008 to include a variety of unique ways to earn lawfully through the site.

Airbnb rental arbitrage is a relatively new strategy in the world of entrepreneurship. It allows hosts to rent out rental spaces to Airbnb guests and is popular among business owners.

Airbnb arbitrage is an innovative technique to investing, however it is used by a tiny number of actual investors.

Airbnb arbitrage, a relatively new type of investment, allows investors to create passive income without taking on the risk of acquiring property.

Arbitrage is one strategy that consumers may use to make Airbnb work for them (and their wallets).

If you can afford to lease or rent a site in a relatively high-trafficked area, you can transform your original investment (the sum paid to rent it out for a month) into considerably more money.

This eliminates the costs, repairs, and responsibilities that come with owning a rental property.

Arbitrage is the technique of profitably selling an item in one market while simultaneously selling it in another. This might relate to anything from a fruit delivery to a rental property.

When we talk about "Airbnb arbitrage," we mean the practice of "re-renting" a property to people who use Airbnb for profit.

A landlord leases vacant flats, houses, cabins, and condos, which are subsequently sublet to Airbnb customers on a nightly, weekly, or monthly basis.

Airbnb is a short-term rental platform. The ultimate result is rental income that (hopefully) exceeds the amount required to rent the location on a monthly basis.

In a nutshell, "Airbnb rental arbitrage" refers to the practice of renting out homes purely for the purpose of subletting them on Airbnb.

In other words, if you generate more money than your rent and business expenditures, you can start making money by advertising a property on Airbnb and earning money from it.

Since 1960, home prices have increased at a rate much faster than the median income, making it increasingly difficult to own real estate. As a result, using this method allows you to improve your cash flow without the stress and challenges connected with home ownership.

Assume you pay $2,000 per month in rent for your apartment. You might pay off your rent in slightly less than two weeks if you sublet the same flat through Airbnb for the entire month at a rate of $150 per day.

After you've paid the rent, the remaining days of the month reflect pure profit. Short-term rental arbitrage allows you to increase your income and save money without owning property because it has the potential for a $2,000 profit per month in our case, after deducting potential maintenance and administrative costs.

This is obviously an oversimplification of the situation. Rent management for a short length of time has related expenditures.

Does it seem too wonderful to be true? Yes and nay at the same time The Airbnb rental arbitrage method has the potential to be successful in certain circumstances. It is a terrific approach that many investors use with low-cost rental homes to make extra money for themselves. However, before jumping headfirst into something, you must conduct extensive research and planning.

Why is there such a thing as Airbnb rental arbitrage?

Many people are in need of short-term accommodation on a frequent basis. Hotels can be fairly expensive, particularly in major cities and other popular tourist destinations. Airbnb has successfully filled a market need by offering accommodations at more competitive pricing.

As a result, offering your vacation rental on Airbnb for a daily charge that is greater than the expenses connected with maintaining the home can earn you a large sum of money.

However, the unit's price must still be less than what a person would pay at a hotel in the same area for a comparable room to the one being rented out.

Is it legal?

Airbnb rental arbitrage may or may not be legal in your location, depending on the laws governing short-term rentals. As a result, begin your investigation first. Most of the world's most populous cities are revising their laws governing short-term rentals.

You'll want to make sure that rental options like Airbnb are legal in the city you're thinking about moving to, or that there is no annual limit on the number of nights you may rent out to visitors, whichever comes first.

If renting out vacation homes is legal in your area, you will also need to determine whether your city, township, state, or province needs you to apply for a hospitality license.

After that, determine whether the landlord from whom you are renting the property allows you to arbitrage between long-term and short-term rents. Some landlords include a condition in their leases that expressly specifies that this is not authorized, or that it is permitted only on a case-by-case basis.

You should always seek authorization from your landlord before subletting your apartment; otherwise, you risk being evicted from your tenancy.

Is this considered acceptable by landlords?

However, Airbnb arbitrage chances are not for everyone. Because there is the risk of legal repercussions if you sublease a property without the landlord's permission, you must ensure that you have a documented agreement with your landlord before proceeding with the procedure.

Despite the fact that the vast majority of landlords expressly prohibit subletting, some will make exceptions on a case-by-case basis. Include in your agreement a discussion about Airbnb host protection insurance. This insurance protects you against responsibility for up to a million dollars in third-party claims.

Once you've agreed with your landlord, it's critical that you take the required procedures to guarantee that you're protected and paid in the event of property damage, personal injury, or natural disasters.

You might begin by looking into Airbnb's Host Protection Insurance; alternatively, you can check into some of the other options for guest screening and insurance.

Why Airbnb Arbitrage Makes Sense

Why does Airbnb arbitrage make financial sense? It's not difficult: the rewards on investment outweigh the costs of making it. Let's have a look at some more instances, shall we?

Scenario 1 (Traditional Investing)

An investor in rental property real estate pays $175,000 to buy a house (the transaction normally closes within a month), then another $5,000 on repairs. After the improvements are completed a month later, they will begin looking for a reliable renter to take over the space.

They spend the following two weeks conducting rental application interviews, and once they've found the perfect tenant, they have them sign a six-month renting agreement. They charge the renters $1,200 per month in rent.

After two and a half months of ownership, the owner of the $180,000 rental property has earned $1,200 in returns on their investment. It's hardly the worst thing that might happen, but in light of the significant investment they've just made, it pales in comparison.

Remember that the homeowner is fully responsible for everything that goes wrong with the property during the 6-month lease, whether it's the heating and cooling system, the plumbing, or even a fire.

They expect to earn around $7,200 in rental income over the life of the lease, although this figure does not include any of their outgoing costs. In the great majority of cases, the investor's cap rate falls between 4% and 7%. Not bad, but not really noteworthy.

Scenario 2 (Airbnb Arbitrage)

Assume the tenant in this scenario had the wonderful notion of leveraging the residence as an Airbnb arbitrage opportunity. They owe the landlord $1,200 per month, but they've discovered that they can earn $500 per week by renting out the house on Airbnb.

They obtain permission from the landlord to rent it out on Airbnb and started collecting $2,000 per month for using it right away. With this arrangement, the tenant earns $800 per month (who is now subletting the home to Airbnb guests).

The tenant is still able to make a handsome profit from the first month, the landlord is still paid on time in accordance with the contract that they have with the tenant, the property owner is protected from liability owing to Airbnb's host protection insurance, and the landlord is still paid. It is a win for everyone concerned.

What are the Benefits of Rental Arbitrage?

Using a rental arbitrage plan to manage your business might provide you with a variety of advantages. In reality, many of the world's most successful Airbnb hosts operate their businesses in this manner.

Sean Rakidzich, a highly successful Airbnb operator, Youtuber, and businessman, employed exclusively the rental arbitrage business model to grow his portfolio from zero to over a hundred units.

The following are some of the advantages of rental arbitrage:

1. Little upfront payments required

You won't have to pay thousands of dollars in down payment because you won't be purchasing the house, thus you won't have to make much of an initial investment.

All you need to do to have your house ready to market on Airbnb is pay the first month's rent, a damage deposit, and any additional expenditures for furnishings, bedding, or amenities.

2. Little to no risk

Because you do not own the property, it is the landlord's responsibility to fix the roof if it deteriorates. If the property does not generate enough money from bookings to cover its running expenditures, you have the option to terminate the lease.

3. You will have rapid growth prospects

If you want your business to succeed, it must be scalable, and rental arbitrage gives you that option. The majority of rental arbitrage hosts use channel manager software to aid in the management of several locations.

4. There is less stress associated with bookkeeping

Landlords are in charge of monitoring and paying a wide range of costs, including HOA dues, mortgage, utilities, and maintenance, among others. Instead, the rent arbitrage host is only needed to pay the landlord the monthly rent, which is a single flat rate.

As can be seen, rental arbitrage provides a number of significant advantages that should not be neglected. Any entrepreneur who can establish their business with very little capital outlay, rapidly develop their operations while reducing their risk exposure, and so on will reap enormous profits.

What are some of the disadvantages of using rental arbitrage?

Despite the fact that they provide numerous benefits to the parties concerned, sublease agreements have a number of significant downsides. It is critical to remember that any business model has both pros and negatives, which is especially true in the case of Airbnb.

Here are some of the drawbacks of rental arbitrage:

1. Rent

Regardless of whether or not you have any bookings for the property, your landlord will expect you to pay rent each month. If you pay late or do not pay at all, you risk incurring late fees, losing your home, and potentially even being sued.

2. Damage to the Property

As the leaseholder, you are responsible for paying for any necessary repairs if one of your guests damages the premises, whether the damage was caused accidently or on purpose. In certain cases, Airbnb and/or your insurance carrier may assist in covering the expenses.

3. Leasehold Agreements

You'll need to meet down with the landlord and draft incredibly detailed leasehold agreements to protect not only yourself, but also the landlord and the guests. Having one of these documents created can be an expensive and time-consuming undertaking, and you may require the assistance of an attorney in many circumstances.

4. Requirements for Legality and Permission

You will need to become acquainted with the local regulations, the HOA rules, and, in some cases, obtain permission from the neighbors. Because municipalities, states, and HOA councils do not want Airbnb to pop up everywhere, highly severe laws have been put in place to limit the locations in which short-term rentals can operate. These limitations also limit the amount of rentals available.

Again, every business has both pros and negatives, so do your research, decide which assets are worth taking a chance on, and avoid any properties where you have cause to suspect there may be issues.

Is Airbnb Rental Arbitrage Right for You?

When it comes to running and expanding their enterprises, hosts have a variety of other feasible options. Even while rental arbitrage is a popular strategy, not everyone will gain from it. Let's take a look at the most common forms of business models available for Airbnb rentals.

1. The buy-and-hold investing approach.

This model is used by the vast majority of real estate investors. It teaches you the foundations required to significantly raise your money over the period of several decades.

Some of the benefits of this approach includes;

Appreciation: Historically, real estate prices rise, and as a result, the amount of equity you have in the property rises.

Paying Off Debt: The principal payments you make toward paying off your mortgage will gradually and steadily increase your worth as you strive toward debt repayment.

Tax Breaks: Owning real estate, particularly rental real estate, can result in large tax breaks. Discuss with your tax preparer the numerous tax benefits that may be available to you.

Because you own the real estate, you have greater influence over your organization. As long as you retain full control of your asset, you will never have to worry about being forced out of it.

2. The Commission Model

The commission model is not as popular as other strategies, but it provides some of the benefits of both buy-and-hold investing and rental arbitrage trading.

The commission model entails forming a partnership with a homeowner and distributing the partnership's revenues and/or profits. Homeowners have the option of listing their property on lucrative OTAs such as Airbnb, VRBO, and Homeaway, as well as using it themselves on occasion.

This is a win-win situation for all parties involved. This business model is used by organizations such as Vacasa, which has thousands of homes across North America. There are some upsides to this model, which include;

There is minimal to no risk: Because the homeowner is liable for all expenses related to property maintenance, including any and all payments associated with the original setup.

Immediate Cash Flow: Because you deduct a commission from the entire amount, you are paid immediately each and every time you obtain a reservation.

You have total control over the listing: Because the homeowner does not own the internet listing, they do not have the right to keep the property's online listings if they decide to fire you from managing their property. Even if the homeowner wishes to keep the web listing for themselves, this is the situation. In other words, they would have to restart the process from the beginning.

3. The Co-host Model

This model allows you to become a partner in an Airbnb house that already has a host. Many hosts do not have the time or money to manage the property on their own, so they seek assistance from co-hosts.

Co-hosts are those who have been pre-screened and approved by the host. In terms of how you get paid, this form of doing business is similar to the commission model, but instead of acting on behalf of the homeowner, you will function as the homeowner's agent.

Let's take a look at some of the advantages of the co-host model, shall we?

Little to no risk: Because, like the commission model, the homeowner is responsible for the initial setup and continuing care of the property, there is little to no financial risk.

Instant Cash Flow: While this is dependent on the arrangement struck between you and the homeowner, you will most likely get paid on a monthly basis.

As you can see, extending your Airbnb business may be performed through the use of a range of various business models. Which of these options is best for you is totally dependent on the personal and professional goals you have in mind. Neither of these options is inherently better than the other.

Moving on, let's get back to rental arbitrage model...

Chapter Three

How To Start Making Money With Airbnb Arbitrage

You've seen a few different scenarios, and you now understand the financial advantages of subletting a rental property through Airbnb. Now that we've reviewed the fundamentals of the process, let's go over the specifics of each phase and how you can start making money using Airbnb arbitrage.

The following explains how successful entrepreneurs earn from Airbnb rental arbitrage, as well as some important information you should be aware of.

Market research should be carried out.

Before signing up to become an Airbnb host, it is essential to conduct extensive market research. To begin, you must determine which towns and regions are likely to be of substantial interest to you. If you want to run a profitable vacation rental business, you must find a house in a desirable neighborhood. If this is not the case, ensuring a consistent flow of money from rental properties would be challenging.

If you're still unclear about which locations are worth your time and attention, have a look at this study of the finest places to visit in the United States. Tourist numbers appear to be highest in the busiest cities with the most attractions.

Another important factor to consider is the potential return on investment (ROI) from a vacation rental property. This can be achieved by choosing a property that is closer to the main sites of interest and conveniences (like a metro station or grocery store).

Although buying a home on the outskirts of town may appear to be a more cost-effective option, it is unlikely to boost your chances of success in the short-term rental market.

You can charge a higher nightly rent if you own a property in a popular tourist region. In any case, before making a decision on your investment in a short-term rental property, you should examine the nightly rates of properties in the region that are comparable to the one you are thinking about buying. If you first identify the normal occupancy rate and any potential expenditures associated, you will be able to create an estimate of your earnings and choose the option that is most profitable to you.

Learn about the regulations in your area.

Before you start making money through rental arbitrage, you need investigate local regulations and legislation. It is no secret that a lot of cities have strengthened the regulations and restrictions that apply to short-term rentals in their localities during the last several years. If you're not sure where to start, check out this post, which will give you a rough idea of the rules and regulations you'll need to follow.

Some communities may outright prohibit vacation rentals, while others may place limits on the number of nights they can be rented out in a year. Will you be able to make a substantial profit if you just rent out your house for ninety days out of the year, for example? If you want to avoid going into the red, this is something you should really consider.

In addition, you must consider whether your landlord will allow you to rent out a property through Airbnb or another company that specializes in vacation rentals. In that instance, you run the risk of being evicted from the flat.

Make a list of all expenses, then source for funds.

You could make a lot of money by hosting Airbnb guests in your rental property; however, you'll have to pay some upfront and ongoing costs. Don't sign the lease agreement unless you have all of the information!

Make sure you have a thorough grasp of the upfront fees as well as the regular costs that will be incurred, and think about how you will be associated with the location in the future.

- ✓ Will you spend your weekends here while renting out the rest of the house during the week?
- ✓ Will you be leaving the house and renting it out instead of living in it as your primary residence?
- ✓ Will you live there full-time and only rent out some of the rooms?
- ✓ Do you now have enough money to pay for them in full?

✓ What would you do if the number of bookings through Airbnb did not meet your expectations?

✓ If the monthly rent was your responsibility, would you be able to pay it?

These are all important factors to consider.

Here are some of the expenses you may incur the following:

✓ Expenses for utilities that are not covered by the landlord.

✓ Guests' access to a reliable Wi-Fi network.

✓ Furnishings for the property, if not already included.

✓ Additional sleeping space is available in the case that more visitors are necessary.

✓ The initial deposit as well as the monthly rent.

✓ The costs of hiring a cleaning service (in the event that you do not intend to clean after each individual guest yourself).

✓ Guests' supplies (toiletries, linens, basic kitchen supplies, light bulbs, etc.).

It is critical to evaluate these costs before entering into a long-term leasing agreement. If this is your first trial on vacation rental management, try out a few different scenarios.

What happens if your occupancy rates for the first six months are 10% lower than expected? Consider a hypothetical circumstance in which normal costs such as cleaning, furnishing, and electricity rates are 10-20% higher than expected.

Some of these expenses are tax deductible, so make sure you have enough money to cover all of them before signing the rental agreement.

Find the Right City

In some cities, Airbnb is more popular than in others. Before you sign your own lease, you should be assured that you have chosen the best location to attract the greatest number of Airbnb guests.

The cities with the most residents and the highest housing prices are not always the ones with the most Airbnb earnings. They are more of a center ground representation. These popular Airbnb destinations draw a huge number of tourists, have a low cost of living, and a limited quantity of hotel rooms.

Among the cities with the worst Airbnb cities are Miami, Venice, Berkeley, Oakland, and Houston. Despite the fact that they are popular holiday destinations, there are a lot of Airbnb listings, and mortgages are more expensive.

Before making any commitments, you should first assess whether your city is a viable location for an Airbnb listing. The placement is extremely important!

Prepare Your Apartment for Rental

When you are satisfied with your financial situation, it is time to begin furnishing and decorating the apartment. When it comes to vacation rentals, having a clean apartment is not enough. It is highly recommended that you seek the advice of an interior designer if you do not have a strong eye for design.

Additionally, amenities such as a washing machine and dryer, a television, a crib, a dishwasher, a coffee maker, and free parking would be beneficial. Certain visitors consider these amenities to be an absolute must when looking for a place to stay.

Assuming your investigation yielded accurate results, the next step will be to furnish and decorate the unit. Some hosts and managers prefer to handle this stage entirely on their own. Some people seek the assistance of interior designers.

We'll skip ahead a little because this stage of the arbitrage process is more concerned with aesthetics than with automation at scale. Always remember that guests are willing to pay for certain amenities, so make sure you provide them (or enhance them).

Start leasing

Once you've selected where you want to rent your Airbnb, the next step is to start looking for houses that are currently available for rent near tourist attractions, city centers, or recreational activities.

When looking at available rental properties, envision yourself as an Airbnb tenant seeking for a pleasant, clean, and safe place to stay for one night, one week, or one month.

This will allow you to more effectively evaluate the standard.

The following are some of the key standards that your rental property should meet:

✓ **Monthly rent is reasonable**

It is in your best advantage for your monthly rent to be closer to the low end of the average range for the area in which you live. This allows you to charge more than the rent and yet make a profit. If the monthly rent is too high, it will be difficult to recoup your costs through Airbnb stays, especially if there are less priced options in the vicinity.

✓ The lease is only for a short time

If this is your first foray into Airbnb arbitrage, start with a short lease time (six months is an excellent place to start). This will ensure that you are not stuck with a site for an extended period of time if things do not go as smoothly as you had intended.

✓ A pristine and safe setting

Even if you can find crumbling apartments for rent at incredibly low prices, it is not worth the money you would have to spend refurbishing run-down buildings in order to attract Airbnb visitors. If the area is known to have a high crime rate, many potential tourists may avoid it entirely, as well as your Airbnb listing.

✓ The location is convenient to local attractions

You do not have to choose a location in your city's downtown area; but, it should be adjacent to something that a tourist would want to do, such as surrounding outdoor activities, the downtown area, tourist attractions, and so on. You could put anything like this as a selling point on your Airbnb listing: "Just 1 mile from the downtown convention center!"

✓ A landlord willing to participate in arbitration

When you tell your landlord about your plan to sublet the property on Airbnb, there is always the possibility that they will decide not to rent to you and instead use your plan instead. This can be a difficult situation because they may be uncomfortable with the idea of so many people entering and exiting the home, or they may be complain about possible problems that could arise. Ensure the landlord is in agreement before making any financial commitment or signing the lease.

Determine your Airbnb Rental Prices.

For this phase, you should do some research. To begin, look at the Airbnb listings in the area and the associated costs, keeping in mind that prices rise on weekends, around holidays, and for any local activities.

When you promote your house on Airbnb again, this might help you figure out how much you should charge for it, and you can also establish a pricing for your property in this section by using the Airbnb calculator.

List Your Home on Airbnb

Once you have selected the appropriate location and property, signed the lease, gathered the funds for all of your expenses, and decided how you will price your location, you are ready to begin staging the home and making it ready to list.

To make the home more welcoming to guests, you may need to renovate it or purchase new furniture (while adhering to your landlord's guidelines). Ensure that there are adequate areas for sitting, sleeping, and lighting, as well as a large quantity of requirements and basic supplies in the house.

The following is a step-by-step guide to listing your property on Airbnb:

✓ Take photos of the property and include a detailed description of its condition in your listing. Highlight any nearby local centers, attractions, or recreational opportunities. Listing the home on Airbnb is free.

✓ You can choose the days, the check-in and check-out times, any additional fees, the required number of nights, the daily fees, and more. You will also be able to list any additional criteria that you have imposed on your guests during this phase.

✓ Submit your listing and make it visible to the public; now, potential guests may examine your lodgings and contact you directly if they want to make a reservation.

Be Available to Guests

Formal Event Authorized Manager Employees wearing credentials and greeting guests at the hotel entry Event Planner Coordinator PR Specialist Employee at Formal Event

You don't have to put in a lot of hours, but you should make sure that you can be reached by your customers whenever they need you. When they check in, ask them if there is anything else you can do for them. Keep a few cots and/or pull-out beds on hand for guests who specifically request them.

Make sure they can contact you in the middle of the night. If you do not believe you will be able to respond immediately whenever a visitor requires assistance from you, find a reliable person who can assist you in dividing the responsibility.

Building a successful Airbnb business necessitates a strong emphasis on delivering outstanding customer service and being responsive to the needs of visitors; otherwise, even a fantastic house in an ideal location risks losing its attraction to potential purchasers.

Optimize Your Listing to Improve Visibility

You won't be able to make a fortune through rental arbitrage if you don't attempt to improve your rating on vacation rental sites; in fact, you should make every effort to attract more visitors to your ad and more tourists to your rental property.

Before you post your listing online, double-check that every component, from the images to the description of your host profile, is up to par. Read this comprehensive guide to learn how to improve your listing and maximize its potential.

If you put in the work, you may increase the exposure of your listing and, as a result, earn more reservations.

Consider developing a website that allows for direct bookings.

After you have received reservations through listing sites and OTAs, it is time to build a direct booking site (DBS) for your business. A DBS is an excellent alternative to the traditional method of paying listing sites commissions.

Furthermore, it is an excellent method for attracting repeat customers and securing your source of income. You can reclaim control of your property and eliminate Airbnb as a potential source of "Airbnb arbitrage" by using a DBS.

Automate Your Rental Arbitrage Business

Property management is a difficult job that can take up a lot of your time and effort. Airbnb hosts are frequently unable to scale their businesses because they are overwhelmed by the number and complexity of the duties they must complete. However, becoming more tech-savvy and utilizing the various tools available for business automation could save your life.

You could start by using vacation rental software to streamline communication with your guests, synchronize your calendars, and plan out your cleaning schedule.

You'll also need these tools to automate and scale your arbitrage business.

Property Management System: software used to distribute content across multiple channels, streamline interactions with guests, delegate tasks, and perform analytics (and much more).

A good property management system (PMS), will also allow you to integrate additional software. The PMS will be the heart of your business operations.

Dynamic pricing app: It enables you to optimize your rental rates in accordance with market dynamics. This program is compatible with your PMS system. This program enables you to "set it and forget it," and it more than pays for itself.

Cleaning coordination software: If you want to hire cleaners or outsource this process, these apps will save you hours of effort. Cleaning management software. Integration is also available between your PMS and cleaning apps. Alternatively, you could try using the PMS's automated functions to accomplish the same thing.

Payment processor: To accept payments from some listing sites, you will need to use a payment processor. In order to accept direct bookings, you must also have a payment processor, such as Stripe or PayPal.

Digital guidebook: It is a low-cost and straightforward solution to create. This technique will be used to transmit check-in instructions, as well as home laws and recommendations.

Naturally, there are numerous software add-ons that will make your task easier. The list shown so far is simply the beginning. Once your business is up and running and you've gained some experience, there will be a lot more that can be done using automation.

Other automation ideas include the following:

- Check-in and check-out systems that are automated
- Utilization of smart amenities (a digital welcome book, smart thermostat, etc.)
- Automating bookkeeping

You will not only be able to increase the efficiency of your business activities, but you will also be able to improve the experience of your guests and produce more revenue through rental arbitrage.

Chapter Four

Startup costs for an Airbnb rental arbitrage business in the United Kingdom

You should budget anywhere between £3,000 and £5,000 for this endeavor. This sum includes the deposit, furnishings, and amenities, as well as the legal paperwork and LLC incorporation.

However, doesn't this contradict the notion that rental arbitrage has a low initial investment? However, these estimates vary greatly depending on location. Depending on your circumstances and the type of property you lease, you may be able to engage in rental arbitrage at a lower cost than this.

Nonetheless, this sum is far more manageable than spending tens of thousands of dollars on a brand new home and getting a mortgage. Furthermore, you will not be responsible for the costs of property maintenance and will not be saddled with debt for an extended period of time.

However, this does not imply that one can engage in rental arbitrage with no or very little money. There will be some upfront costs that you will need to consider, so it is highly recommended that you keep some extra cash on hand at all times. If reservations do not come in right away, this will help pay off the lease during the off-season when the space is not in use.

> **Rental deposits are the first expense.**

A security deposit on the apartment will be one of the first significant costs. You will need financial resources to enter into a long-term lease agreement with the landlord. As a result, in addition to paying the first and last month's rent, you will be required to pay a security deposit. In some cases, you may be able to persuade the landlord to accept the first month's rent as the security deposit instead.

> ### The second cost is for furniture.

Whenever possible, you should try to rent a house that is at least partially furnished. Because it is possible that someone who owns a fully furnished home is also renting it out on a short-term basis. Furthermore, the cost of fully furnishing a new home may add anywhere between £3,000 and £5,000 to the initial capital required.

If the apartment is only partially furnished, your best bet is to go shopping for low-cost items. You can save money on materials by shopping at places like Home Depot or IKEA. If you look carefully enough, you might find a hidden treasure at Walmart.

> ### Next comes expenses for photographic services

You must take care of it! The cameras on iPhones are excellent. Do-it-yourself photography is an excellent way to save money.

> ➤ **Cleaning services are the fourth expense.**

This is already included in the starting pricing, but you will have to pay for professional cleaning services in the long run. If you have the requisite expertise and skills, doing things yourself from the start is the most effective way to decrease costs and save money.

If you've never done it before or don't want to spend the time learning how to clean a house. If this is the case, hiring a cleaning service is your best bet. This could cost you anywhere between fifty and two hundred and fifty pounds, depending on the size and location.

> ➤ **Legal consultation constitutes expense number five**

Maintaining a cordial working relationship with a Real Estate attorney may be quite beneficial for those in the

Airbnb business. Because Airbnb's regulations are constantly changing, you will need legal counsel to successfully adapt your business to comply with them.

If you have any legal issues with the landlord or guests, they can also be of great help to you. In the event that something unfortunate occurs, they can help you file damage claims and obtain insurance.

Chapter Five

How to Calculate the Rental Arbitrage Return on Investment (ROI)

At the end of the day, you got into this business to make more money than you put in. In the right markets, the return on investment (ROI) of a rental arbitrage property can be quite lucrative.

However, as with any other type of business, the return on investment (ROI) will vary depending on factors such as location, initial investment, ongoing costs, and a variety of other considerations.

ROI is computed by dividing the investment cost by the net return on investment.

Here is an example of a simple rental arbitrage transaction:

Initial Investments

Expense	Cost ($)
First Month's Rent	1,000
Damage Deposit	500
Furniture	2,500
Décor	1,000
Total	5,000

Annual Operating Costs

Expense	Cost ($)
Rent	12,000
Cleaner's Pay	4,500
Maintenance	1,200
Licenses Permits	300
Utilities	3,600
Total	21,600

Annual Revenue from Bookings

Revenue

Bookings	22,000
Cleaning Fees	4,500
Total	26,500

Annual Revenue from Bookings - Annual Operating Expenses = Net Return on Investment

Annual Profit = $4,900

ROI = (Start-up Costs / Annual Profit) X 100%

This gives,

ROI = ($5,000 / $4,900) X 100% Annual

Therefore,

ROI = 98%

How to Find Your First Rental Arbitrage Property

While discussing rental arbitrage can be entertaining, actually engaging in it can be difficult if you are unsure of how to get started. To help you get started, we have compiled a few pointers.

Join real estate investor Facebook groups: Communicate with other investors in your area, and share with them how you can help them improve their financial status.

Create a Website: Using a website to advertise your services will immediately boost your trustworthiness, and if done effectively, landlords will approach you regarding available homes!

Networking Events: Real estate investors can discover networking opportunities in every major city; attend those events on a regular basis and chat to the investors there to see if any of them would be interested in collaborating on a business venture.

Cold calling: Cold calling is still effective today, believe it or not. Pick up the phone and call potential landlords to inquire about the possibility of subletting the space to you.

Methods for Finding Properties Suitable for Rental Arbitrage

1. Look for the most trustworthy rental listing websites.

This way, you will have an easier time distinguishing the properties that are located in the location that you select, as well as viewing the additional categories, such as the square footage and amenities that are associated with the properties.

The three most highly recommended listing websites are:

✓ Apartments.com; it is a well-known rental service that provides simple options for do-it-yourself landlords and smaller property management companies.

✓ Zillow

✓ Zumper

2. Look online for landlords who are ok with Airbnb rental arbitrage.

Despite the fact that some landlords may consider subletting to be illegal, there are undoubtedly a large number of owners who do not prohibit it. You can search for apartments to sublease using search engines like Google or Facebook marketplace, or you can go straight to Craigslist and begin your search there!

3. Attend local real estate investor meetings and form new partnerships.

If you use networking to find out if they have any leads on the property you are looking for, you will have a much easier time getting a nice pitch together and meeting people. You can also go to meetup.com, key in the name of the city you're most interested in, and immediately begin searching for events and meetings relating to real estate!

4. Speak to local real estate agents

Discuss your plans with local real estate professionals in order to find the best rental property to use as an arbitrage opportunity.

It is not difficult to find local real estate agents if you look at the top real estate websites or search the internet for them. You owe it to them to tell them the truth about your plans to launch a rental arbitrage business.

Tell them that one of your goals over the next six months is to manage more than 20 homes. Because you have the potential to become a large source of income for realtors, this type of pitching is effective when done with them.

The most recommended website for this is realtor.com. In fact, it is affiliated with the National Association of Realtors.

Trulia, the best mobile app, allows you to look for real estate homes in an easy and convenient manner.

5. Speak with Airbnb hosts.

Make an effort to contact Airbnb hosts whose listings have no reviews, poor images, and inadequate descriptions, and it would be ideal if their host response rate was less than 50%. These hosts are typically homeowners who are willing to rent out their homes on a short-term basis, but the money they make from doing so is not particularly lucrative.

You may approach them and tell them that you can provide them with a guaranteed monthly income for the next 12 to 24 months, and they could find the idea interesting.

How to Persuade Your Landlord to Agree to an Airbnb Rental Arbitrage

You've determined where you want to start your Airbnb business, and you've investigated the policies and procedures that are required in that city; the next step is to find a landlord who will allow you to rent their property and then utilize it as a short-term rental property.

You will discover that the most difficult aspect of Airbnb rental arbitrage is convincing landlords to rent to you.

After all, you always run the risk of your landlord changing their mind about renting to you after you inform them of your intention to use Airbnb as a rental platform, and if they do, you will no longer be able to rent their property.

How can you do this?

The two key considerations that contribute to enterprising tenants' reluctance to discuss this arrangement with their landlord are as follows:

✓ They could say no; and

✓ It's probable that they'll copy their renter's concept and list the house on Airbnb rather than leasing it out.

As a result, if you want to persuade your landlord to let you do this, you must address their concerns and demonstrate that the agreement benefits them by convincing them that;

> **You Will Maintain the Unit in Excellent Condition**

If you want to receive five-star ratings for the flat, you must keep it tidy and possibly even Instagram-worthy at all times. A well-maintained rental property can save its owner time and money that would otherwise be spent on maintenance and improvements.

> **You Will Make Payments on Time**

Because you want to manage the rental property as a lucrative business, you will be able to ensure that your payments to the landlord are made on time, which may already mean a lot to them given how difficult it is to hunt down tenants and collect their monthly rent payments.

> ➤ **Running a short-term rental business is Hands-On**

Even if your landlord believes that hosting their house directly on Airbnb will earn them more money than signing a long-term lease, you must still demonstrate to them how much effort is required to manage even one Airbnb rental property. We can only hope that they will not want to be bothered by such a large amount of labor and will instead agree to the arbitrage.

Once they have agreed to arbitration, you will need to modify your lease to include a rental arbitrage contract. The following would be included in a template for a rental arbitrage leasing agreement:

✓ Who is in charge of paying any fines or penalties?

- ✓ If liability insurance is required, who will be liable for paying for it?
- ✓ What portion of your profits are you willing to share with your landlord?
- ✓ Are obligated to give your landlord advance notice of any guests, as well as how will communicate about this?
- ✓ Should you pay an additional security deposit if necessary?

> **Ensure the property and gain the landlord's trust.**

From bothering guests troubling landlords, you must ensure that you are using the appropriate tools to ensure that the property is secure and that the neighbors are satisfied.

Many landlords may have issue and complaints like noise complaints and the likes. To help with these issues, you can use some of the tools below;

Simply Safe: Simply Safe refers to a series of home surveillance equipment that can be put within the house to verify that no dubious conduct is going place; make careful to educate guests about them and gain their permission before beginning.

Auto host: It is a mechanism that automatically screens potential tenants for inappropriate behavior.

Alexa Guard: If you already own an Amazon Echo device, you can use the Alexa Guard function to find out when people are organizing parties; it is a built-in feature that monitors variations in sound levels and alerts you if guests are throwing a party and making too much noise.

InsuraGuest: It's an insurance and technology firm, supports you with risk assessment and provides protection beyond what Airbnb and VRBO provide.

Airbnb Calculator: You may set your landlord's mind at ease by offering income forecasts backed up by Airbnb statistics using the Airbnb Calculator.

NoiseAware: It is a system that analyzes environmental noise and offers call center coverage around the clock (they will place calls if things get out of hand).

Because you'll have more than one arbitrage property before you know it, integrating the service into the PMS will provide you with the benefits of coordinating and automating such services at scale.

Chapter Six

Cities in the United States with the biggest profit potential for Airbnb rental arbitrage

The following cities are the best for making money through Airbnb rental arbitrage:

The five cities with the greatest potential for profit via rental arbitrage, taking into account both profit potential and local legislation governing short-term rentals.

1. Annapolis, Maryland

Because of its closeness to Baltimore and Washington, DC, as well as its sailboat races and an eight-acre woodland garden, the state capital of Maryland attracts visitors practically all year. In Anne Arundel County, hosts of short-term stays and rental arbitrage sites such as Airbnb are obliged to register their rental units with the county.

Here are some Airbnb stats for this city;

- Airbnb had a Cash on Cash Return of 6.19%.
- Airbnb's daily cost is $334.
- Airbnb Rental Earnings: $6,943
- Airbnb's occupancy rate is 68%.
- A typical home costs $797,902 at the moment.
- The property is priced at $376 per square foot.
- Days on the market: 108 days.

2. Nashville, Tennessee

Nashville is gradually becoming one of the most popular southern towns to visit, with a wide range of attractions such as live music venues, up-and-coming restaurants, and the Country Music Hall of Fame. It is necessary for hosts to apply for a permit to run a short-term rental property.

Here are the Airbnb stats;

- Airbnb provides a Cash on Cash Return of 5.1%.
- Airbnb charges a daily fee of $255.
- Airbnb Rental Earnings: $3,905
- Airbnb's occupancy rate is 58%.
- The current average price of a property is $509,892.
- The property's asking price is $356 per square foot.
- Days on the market: 65.

3. North Las Vegas, Nevada (USA).

Visitors to the Las Vegas Motor Speedway can enjoy high-octane events and festivals. These events attract visitors to North Las Vegas. Property owners who use their properties for short-term rentals or rental arbitrage on Airbnb must obtain both a conditional use permit and a business license.

Find the Airbnb stats below;

- Airbnb has a Cash on Cash Return of 6.22%.

- Airbnb's daily rate is $273.

- Airbnb Rental Earnings: $3,852

- Airbnb has a 61% occupancy rate.

- The current average price of a home is $410,295

- The property is priced at $219 per square foot.

- Days on the market: 55.

4. Oklahoma City, Oklahoma

Oklahoma City is a tourism hidden gem; the city's rich history, cowboy culture, art, parks, and diverse districts make it a wonderful destination to visit. Home sharing is only permitted in residential areas of the city, and hosts must obtain a home-sharing license for each separate apartment rented out.

Let's check out the stats;

- Airbnb has a Cash on Cash Return of 5.79%.
- Airbnb charges $94 per day.
- $2,669 in Airbnb rental income
- Airbnb's occupancy rate is now 74.86%.
- The median price for a home is $329,991
- The property is priced at $157 per square foot.
- Days on the market: 58.

5. Saint Paul, Minnesota

Visitors come to Saint Paul all year as a direct result of the active tourism activities that are in place. The breathtaking beauty is the main attraction for travelers, especially during the autumn months. Before hosts can legally operate in the city, the city's Department of Safety and Inspections must issue them a Short Term Rental Host license.

Below are the Airbnb stats;

- Airbnb had a Cash on Cash Return of 5.15%.
- On Airbnb, the daily rent is $179.
- $2,846 in Airbnb rental income
- Airbnb's occupancy rate is 64%.
- A residence costs an average of $293,336.
- The property is priced at $204 per square foot.
- Days on the market: 58.

Locations in the United Kingdom with the Best Rental Arbitrage Potential

Northern Headquarters, the Baltic Triangle, and Chinatown are some of the first places that come to mind when one thinks of the United Kingdom. Let's have a look at two of the most favorable locations in the UK for rental arbitrage:

1. Jericho

According to Airbtics investigation, Jericho is the greatest place to start a Rental Arbitrage organization. On Airbnb, there are more than 67 listings, with 16 for private rooms and 17 for homes with one bedroom. The majority of the properties had a monthly revenue of more than $4,107 and an occupancy rate of more than 89%.

2. The New Town of Edinburgh

According to Airbtics, Edinburgh New Town is the second-best market in which to build a Rental Arbitrage business. There are presently over 509 listings available on Airbnb, including 127 one-bedroom residences and 80 private room listings. The bulk of properties have a monthly revenue of more than $4,679 and an occupancy rate of more than 84%.

Chapter Seven

The Most Essential Requirements for a Successful Airbnb Arbitrage

The ideal formula for profit will be defined to a large extent by the goals you want to achieve with your business. Calculating the weighted average rate that applies to your location, on the other hand, can give you a general idea of whether or not you will be able to make a profit.

The following is the formula:

1. Determine the weekly and weekend rates for daily rentals in your location, and then take an average of those rates.

You can locate rentals on Airbnb that provide you access to this information. Simply conduct a search for comparable properties in your neighborhood and keep track of their prices during the week and on weekends. Keep everything in a spreadsheet to make life easier.

2. Determine the weighted average price for each property.

Weighted Average Airbnb Rate = (Weekday Average Airbnb Rate * 5 + Weekend Average Airbnb Rate * 2) / 7

For example, if the average rate for a stay on Airbnb during the week is $50 and the average rate for a weekend stay is $100, the Weighted Average Airbnb Rate is $64 because ($50 * 5 + $100 * 2) / 7 = $64.

3. Calculate the daily cost of all expenses for your property.

Take the total amount you spent on your property each month and divide it by 30 to get the daily cost of your property.

If the total cost of maintaining your property (including rent and any fees) is $2,000 per month, the daily cost of your property expenses is $67.

4. Divide the weighted average price of your Airbnb listing by the daily cost.

The final ratio is calculated by dividing the weighted average of the daily property costs by the weighted average rate. It will help you determine the minimum number of days per month that your home must be rented out to generate a profit.

In this example, the final ratio is $64/$67, which is 0.95.

This means that in order to generate a return on your real estate investment, you must rent it out for the majority of the month.

If, on the other hand, this ratio is equal to or greater than one, it indicates that you can make a profit even if you rent out the property for fewer days per month.

If the Weighted Average Airbnb Price is, for instance, $125 and your Property Expenses by Day are still $67, the Final Ratio is 1.87 ($125/$67), indicating that you will be able to start turning a profit in less than one month.

If at all possible, you should try to arbitrage a piece of real estate with a Final Ratio of 2.0 or higher. If you aim for a higher Final Ratio, you'll give yourself more leeway. If you proceed in this manner, you will be able to guarantee that you will not lose money on your property each month.

Chapter Eight
Risks Involved In Airbnb Rental Arbitrage

If you intend to invest in Airbnb rental arbitrage, you should be aware of the potential risks. The following is a list of some of the most serious dangers to be aware of:

➤ **Changes in Market Conditions**

Recognize that market conditions are constantly changing. As a result, the amount of interest shown in booking your home can vary significantly from month to month. You are still vulnerable to the shifting currents of the overall housing market, just like in traditional real estate leasing arrangements.

➤ Local Rules and Regulations

If you intend to rent a condominium or apartment unit in the city where you live, you must ensure that you are in compliance with local city regulations.

The rules of your Homeowners' Association (HOA) may also limit your ability to rent out your property on a short-term basis. Before you buy or rent a new property, you must ensure that you are familiar with and follow these requirements.

➤ Unexpected Occurrences

Will you be able to make a profit on the sale of your house if you are unable to rent it out for a few months? What would you do if your area was hit by a natural disaster? It is critical to consider all potential hazards when calculating how much profit your Airbnb business must generate in order to avoid going into the red.

➤ Unstable Income Sources

Will the changing of the seasons affect how much money you make through Airbnb? This question must be answered before you choose a location for your business.

Bookings may increase significantly in some months, but revenue may decrease significantly in others. Even if your business is prone to seasonality, you can still exert control over your earnings by developing unique promotions and deals for your customers.

Conclusion

Should You Participate in Airbnb Arbitrage?

Because you do not need to own a home to become an Airbnb host, making money through Airbnb arbitrage is becoming more frequent. If you conduct significant market research and obtain the necessary approvals, you will be able to pay your rent and have the possibility to become a successful full-time host.

Arbitrage on Airbnb is a great strategy to consider, especially if you want to get into the real estate business but only have a small amount of your own money to invest. Despite the fact that not everyone should do it, the potential benefits are enormous.

You can go a step further and automate your business to improve the quality of the experience your customers have when they visit your establishment. If you can reduce the amount of time you spend on routine tasks, you will have more opportunities to grow your business and, as a result, your income from vacation rentals.

"House sharing" is becoming increasingly popular as more people choose not to stay in hotels. You have the potential to profit from this trend; however, before diving headfirst into this endeavor, ensure you have a thorough understanding of the risks involved.

Have a prosperous business!

Made in the USA
Middletown, DE
16 April 2023